Aug 16

FOOTSTEPS TO FREEDOM

THE UNDERGROUND RAILROAD

THE NEED FOR FLIGHT

CLAIRE O'NEAL

PURPLE TOAD
PUBLISHING

FOOTSTEPS TO
FREEDOM
THE UNDERGROUND RAILROAD

FAMOUS FIGHTERS by Wayne L. Wilson
FREE AT LAST—OR WERE THEY? by Claire O'Neal
THE NEED FOR FLIGHT by Claire O'Neal
GOING UNDERGROUND by Amie Jane Leavitt

Copyright © 2016 by Purple Toad Publishing, Inc.

PUBLISHER'S NOTE

The *Footsteps to Freedom: The Underground Railroad* series covers slavery and racism in United States history. Some of the events told in this series may be disturbing to young readers. The data in this book has been researched in depth, and to the best of our knowledge is factual. Although every measure is taken to give an accurate account, Purple Toad Publishing makes no warranty of the accuracy of the information and is not liable for damages caused by inaccuracies.

ABOUT THE AUTHOR

Claire O'Neal has written over thirty books for children. She holds degrees in English and Biology from Indiana University, and a PhD in Chemistry from the University of Washington. She loves reading and writing, and especially learning more about history and culture. Claire lives with her husband and two sons in Delaware.

Printing   1   2   3   4   5   6   7   8   9

Publisher's Cataloging-in-Publication Data
O'Neal, Clare.
    The Need for Flight / written by Clare O'Neal.
    p. cm.
        Includes bibliographic references and index.
        ISBN 9781624692178
1. Underground Railroad—Juvenile literature. 2. Antislavery movements—United States—Juvenile literature. I. Series: Footsteps to Freedom The Underground Railroad.
E450 2016
973.7115

CONTENTS

CHAPTER 1

BOUGHT AND SOLD

Solomon Northup lived a rare and happy life in Saratoga, New York. A professional and respected musician, Solomon's violin sang before adoring audiences. His performances earned him enough money to live in a comfortable home with his wife, Anne, and three children. Solomon was black, a free man, the son of a freed slave.

In 1841, two white businessmen, Alexander Merrill and Joseph Russell, came to Solomon, seeking his talents to perform with a traveling circus around Washington, D.C. The three struck a deal. Solomon traveled with the men to Washington, stopping at several restaurants along the way. The journey made him unwell—was it something he ate or drank? That night at the hotel, his head pounded and he couldn't sleep. People urged him to come with them to the doctor. It was the last thing he could remember.

Beams of light suddenly pierced Solomon's thick sleep, breaking through

Solomon Northup and other slaves wore loose work clothes made of cheap material as they worked cotton and sugarcane fields on Edwin Epps's plantation near Bayou Boeuf, Louisiana.

Slave pens held slaves in shackles or cages lined with hay—like farm animals—as they awaited trading or auction. In 1865, black Union soldiers posed with the empty Birch's slave pen in Alexandria, Virginia.

cracks in boarded-up windows. He was not at the hotel. A musty smell of hay, mixed with sweat and fear, jolted him awake. The soft mattress and his pillow were gone, replaced by a hard dirt floor and a rough wooden fence. Heavy iron chains were attached to locked shackles on his wrists and ankles. He couldn't stand up, much less walk away. Solomon's head spun with sleep and confusion.

"Where am I?" he croaked, to no one in particular.

A black man answered, rough and defeated, chained right behind him. "In the Williams Slave Pen. Ain't no use in struggling. Them chains ain't coming off. You about to be sold."

Panic jolted Solomon awake. "*What?* No! I'm a free man!"

A white man entered. Now there would be answers. "Sir, why am I chained? I demand that you remove these irons from me!"

James H. Birch was a slave dealer. He merely smiled and replied, "None of my business, son."

Solomon knew his rights. "But sir, I am a *free man* and I have papers to prove it. I was born in Essex County, New York, and my name is—"

"Rodbury!" Birch called, and a strong white man entered. Relief washed over Solomon as they worked with his chains. But Rodbury did not set him free. Instead, he led Solomon to a bench and held him tight by his wrists. Solomon struggled and fought as the two tore his shirt from his back. Solomon heard Birch breathing over him. Then *whack!* Surprise, shock, *pain.* Again and again, Birch struck Solomon's back with a wooden paddle. He stopped only when the paddle broke. As Solomon's back burned, Birch fetched a cat-o'-nine-tails, a whip with nine stinging ends. He lashed Solomon's back one hundred times. Solomon was raw, bleeding, and nearly unconscious from pain. Birch finally stopped, then he leaned down and spoke, dangerous and soft, in Solomon's ear, *"If you tell anyone you are a free man, I swear I will kill you."*[1]

Solomon Northup, born a free man, had been kidnapped and sold into slavery for $625. His misery had just begun. He was herded onto a steamboat along with 48 other black men, women, and even children as young as seven years old. All would be sold at the slave auctions in New Orleans.

First, Solomon was bought by William Ford, a carpenter and businessman. Ford treated Solomon kindly, but sold him after a year to Edwin Epps. Solomon spent 11 years toiling on the Epps cotton plantation in Bayou Boeuf, Louisiana. Epps was a cruel master who beat his slaves for fun, or worse, demanded that they beat each other while he watched.

And yet Northup was lucky. He spent twelve years as a slave in Louisiana, but with the help of a Canadian friend, Samuel Bass, Northrup wrote to

Attorney Henry B. Northup helped free his relative Solomon Northup.

Solomon and his wife and children shared an emotional reunion after twelve years apart.

lawyers in New York, asking them to fight for his freedom. New York Governor Washington Hunt even wrote letters on his behalf. In January of 1853, Northup embraced his wife and children once more. He spent the rest of his life in peace.

Millions of other black Americans knew no such happy ending. For them, their lives were spent working for someone else each day, until their hands were raw and their feet bled, only to wake the next day to do it all over again. Theirs was a life of pain and fear—a life without hope—all because of the color of their skin.

Southerners called slavery a "peculiar institution." Many whites believed slavery was necessary to help farm the rich land in the young country. Slavery in America began when the first 20 slaves arrived in the Jamestown colony in 1619 aboard a Dutch West India trading ship. It ended with the passage of the 13th Amendment banning slavery in 1865. Finally, the 14th Amendment granted former slaves citizenship in 1868. Two hundred and fifty years of America's history was built on the backs of millions of African Americans who suffered terrible cruelties that we may never fully understand.

Slavery and the Constitution

The early leaders of the United States needed to address slavery when they wrote the U.S. Constitution in 1787. The South—its landowners, its trade and businesses—was completely dependent on the cheap labor of slaves to run its farms. Southern states would never agree to ban slavery outright. But at the same time, slavery had recently been outlawed in other countries, including Great Britain and Portugal. Slavery was becoming increasingly unpopular in the North. As they wrote Article 1 of the Constitution, legislators struck a compromise. Article 1, Section 2 states that slaves would be counted toward a state's population—not as whole people, but rather each slave as 3/5ths of a person. To satisfy the North, Article 1, Section 9 states that importing slaves from overseas would become illegal beginning in 1808. Neither idea was perfect. Americans would later use the "3/5ths Compromise" as proof that blacks could never be full citizens. And plantation owners hurried to import tens of thousands of slaves during the final two decades of the legal Atlantic slave trade, more than any other period in colonial history.

Slaves sold at auction, like these men in South Carolina, were chained together by their necks, wrists, or feet to keep them from running away.

SLAVERY COMES TO AMERICA

Black slaves were first brought out of Africa when Spanish and Portuguese explorers began sailing the continent's west coast in the fifteenth century. They watched African chiefs trading their prisoners of war, caught in tribal battle, as slaves. Encouraged by Prince Henry of Portugal, the sailors soon found that African slaves brought valuable prices at markets, just like other African goods, such as nuts, fruit, oils, and gold.

After Portugal, the Dutch and then the British took turns as world leaders in buying and selling Africans as slaves. These white men looked different and spoke different languages. How could they get Africans to board their strange, huge ships? First, slave traders would meet with a friendly local African, the caboceer, who knew how to gather unsuspecting people and bring them to the coast. Some caboceers had tricks up their sleeves. American slave Richard Jones told of a man who came to his grandmother's village one day and showed everyone a scrap of soft red fabric. The villagers rushed

African caboceers or even tribal chiefs helped European slave merchants find, trap, and kidnap their own people in exchange for valuable goods.

to grab such a rare gift. The man laid down another scrap, farther away. The villagers followed. The man soon decorated a path with red scraps. The excited villagers followed, all the way up a plank and onto a riverboat bound for the slaving coast.[1] But capture wasn't usually so quiet. Charles Ball's grandfather awoke one morning to find his village filled with screams. Enemies surrounded his family, his friends, and his neighbors. They beat his people with clubs and spears and shot with arrows those who ran.[2]

Those who did not escape were tied or chained together and forced to march to the coast. The long and difficult journey sometimes took weeks as the captives walked endlessly through forests and over rivers. They might be bought and sold several different times, traded for valuable goods like guns, colorful cotton and fabrics, metals and ivory, or alcoholic drinks.

Newly captured Africans walked in human caravans, sometimes as far as 1,000 miles, to be sold as slaves on the coast.

St. George Castle, built by the Portuguese in 1482, served as an important trading post for African slaves. It still stands in Elmina, Ghana.

Waiting for them on the coast were sturdy forts known as "slave castles." Many people would be shackled and kept as prisoners in these human warehouses to wait for ships to arrive from across the Atlantic. Women and children were allowed to roam freely within their prison, while men—the more valuable slaves—were chained or bound together with rope. Soldiers stood guard to prevent the living merchandise from escaping. Many Africans had never before laid eyes on white people. To slave Charles Ball's grandfather, "white people . . . appeared to me the ugliest creatures in the world."[3]

Finally, a huge ship arrived to take the Africans on the Middle Passage—their journey across the ocean to America. Sea captains chained the people together by their hands and feet. They led them into the ship's belly to dark windowless decks, with ceilings so low that slaves had to stoop, sit, or lie down. Men, women,

Slaves were starved and trapped in cramped quarters during the Middle Passage. The sea voyage took between one and six months, depending on the weather.

and children were crammed together in a space smaller than a coffin. Some suffocated. Many died from diseases that spread quickly in the cramped quarters. The health of their cargo did not worry the slave traders, who fed them as little as possible and often gave them dirty water to drink.

Captains beat and abused their captives at any time, for any reason. Historians estimate that nearly 2 million Africans died during the Middle Passage, whether from ill-treatment, illness, or even suicide by jumping overboard. Of the estimated 12.5 million Africans taken from their home during the slave trade between 1525 and 1866, however, most did survive the Middle Passage. When they reached the New World, they were sold into a lifetime of slavery.[4]

Rebellions often broke out on slave ships. By taking over the ship, slaves could take their lives back. What did they have to lose? One such ship, the *Amistad*, was

transporting 53 Africans to the Caribbean. On July 1, 1839, an African named Cinqué led the prisoners on board to break free and steal the sailors' knives. The Africans killed all of their captors except the two who could sail them back home to Africa. But the sailors tricked the slaves and sailed northwest to the United States instead.

The U.S. Navy captured the *Amistad* just outside of New York City. The Navy imprisoned the African rebels in New Haven, Connecticut, on charges of murder, while the sailors were set free. Eventually, the murder charges were dropped, but the Africans sat in prison while the U.S. government decided what to do with them. President Martin Van Buren wanted to send them to their original destination

The Spanish ship *La Amistad* (Spanish for "Friendship") carried African slaves bound for the sugar plantations of Cuba.

Joseph Cinqué (1814–1879) originally came from the Mende people of Sierra Leone. He returned to his homeland and lived the rest of his life there, where he was also known as Sengbe Pieh.

in Cuba. Abolitionists, who wanted slavery to be outlawed, disagreed. The argument went all the way to the Supreme Court in January 1841, where former U.S. president John Quincy Adams defended the Africans' freedom.

The case was a victory for Cinqué and the *Amistad* Africans. In the end, 35 of the *Amistad* captives, including Cinqué, returned to their African homeland. Eighteen others had already died, either at sea or in prison awaiting trial.

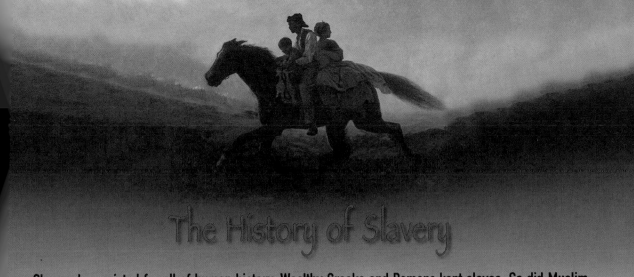

The History of Slavery

Slavery has existed for all of human history. Wealthy Greeks and Romans kept slaves. So did Muslim populations of Africa and the Middle East. In these societies, as in Africa, prisoners captured in battle often became household servants. They helped on the small family farm or with household chores and duties. If they spoke a different language or practiced a different religion, their masters generally allowed them to keep those customs alive. It was often possible, too, for servants to work toward their freedom.

The African slave trade was unique in several ways. African slaves were captured, bought, and sold to work on huge plantations of cash crops in the New World. Most African slaves were taken to the Caribbean or South America, where they toiled in sugarcane and cotton fields, treated brutally by masters and overseers. But they were allowed to keep their culture and community alive. In fact, African languages influenced Caribbean dialects; African music and dance helped to define Caribbean rhythms. African religions and beliefs can be seen even today in Caribbean art, customs, and festivals.[5]

In total, only 5 percent of captured Africans were taken to the United States.[6] These slaves were stripped, not just of their clothes, but of their history, their language, their religion, their music, and even their names.[7]

A slave carries a heavy wine jug in an ancient Roman mosaic.

CHAPTER 3

SLAVERY IN THE NORTH

Isabella Baumfree was unlucky to live in New York, one of the last Northern states to abolish slavery. She was born to two slave parents in the village of Hurley around 1797. At nine years old, Belle was torn from her parents and sold to John Neely for $100, along with a flock of sheep. Neely beat her severely before he sold her to a restaurant owner. Belle's fifth and final master, John Dumont, loved her. His jealous wife insisted Belle be forced to marry another slave, Thomas, so that Dumont would forget her.

Belle was 30 when the state of New York outlawed slavery. Suddenly she was free! But two of her children were not. They still owed years of work to the Dumonts to earn their freedom. Belle stole her infant daughter, Sophia, and marched down to court. Though she was black, and a woman, she was not afraid to demand that her five-year-old son Peter be returned to her, after Mr. Dumont had sold him illegally into slavery in Alabama.

Born a slave, Sojourner Truth (1797–1883) became famous as a free woman for her bravery in speaking up for the rights of blacks and women.

Was it her fiery words? Her nearly 6-foot-tall frame? Belle's bold move worked. She and Peter were reunited, but not before her son's new master had whipped him so much that he bore scars from head to toe for the rest of his life.

Belle never learned how to read or write, but she had a powerful voice and a burning message to deliver. On June 1, 1843, she claimed she heard the voice of God. She told her friends, "The Spirit calls me, and I must go." Belle changed her name to Sojourner Truth—a traveler (sojourner), preaching justice for God. Sojourner journeyed across the country, to New York City, Massachusetts, Ohio, even as far away as Michigan, speaking out against slavery and also for women's rights. She had a way with words that made audiences sit up and listen.

Sojourner became an important black voice for white abolitionists. They wanted slavery outlawed, but sometimes for complicated reasons. Some practical Northerners worried that the cheap labor provided by slaves would push working

■ FREE STATES   ☐ SLAVE STATES

By 1860, 15 states allowed slavery, while 18 states, including the new states of Oregon and California, did not. The Missouri Compromise of 1820 outlawed slavery in territories above 36 degrees 30 minutes latitude.

The Massachusetts Anti-Slavery Society encouraged its members to donate pennies at a time. The loose change paid for anti-slavery newsletters and abolitionist speakers at events.

whites out of jobs. Some religious men and women, especially Quakers, believed that slavery was not Christian. To them, slavery conflicted with the important American ideal that "all men are created equal." They felt that the Declaration of Independence protected the rights of blacks as well as whites.

Most whites disagreed. They told themselves that they were better in all ways than blacks. Most whites everywhere, South *and* North, believed that blacks could never be intelligent or good-looking, or even able to love or have deep and meaningful feelings. Yet talented black people all around them proved them wrong every day.

Phillis Wheatley was born in Africa. She was only seven or eight years old when slave traders snatched her from her village. She remembered her beautiful, warm mother, who welcomed the sun each day by pouring water on the ground outside their hut. Her people were farmers and traders, dancers and musicians. They wrote no history, but spoke it instead, weaving their stories into a poetry that brought its own music to a village fireside. Phillis carried that poetry inside her all her life, even after she was sold into slavery to John Wheatley in Boston.

Phillis was far luckier than most. It was against the law for black children to attend school. Wheatley's children, Mary and Nathaniel, tutored her in English, Latin, geography, history, and astronomy. Her education put her far ahead of even most white children.

Phillis's natural gift for words led her to write whole books of her own poetry. Many outside the family could not believe that a black person, let alone a woman, could write so well. Phillis had to take a test in front of prominent Boston men,

The City of Boston dedicated this sculpture of Phillis Wheatley in 2003, as part of the Boston Women's Memorial along Commonwealth Avenue.

Phillis Wheatley's collection of poetry, *Poems on Various Subjects, Religious and Moral,* was published in London in 1773.

including John Hancock, who would later sign the Declaration of Independence, to prove to everyone that her work was her own.

She soon became a celebrated poet in Boston. The Wheatley family published her collection of poems in London. They even took Phillis there, where she met the Lord Mayor of London and many figures in Great Britain's high society. Her poetry was so well received that London newspapers harshly criticized the Wheatley family for not granting Phillis's freedom, which they did in late 1773.

POEMS

ON

VARIOUS SUBJECTS,

RELIGIOUS AND MORAL.

BY

PHILLIS WHEATLEY,

NEGRO SERVANT to Mr. JOHN WHEATLEY, of BOSTON, in NEW ENGLAND.

LONDON:

Printed for A. BELL, Bookseller, Aldgate; and sold by Messrs. COX and BERRY, King-Street, BOSTON.

MDCCLXXIII.

Phillis belonged to an especially kind master. But even the average slave experienced a very different life in the North than in the South. Northern slaveowners rarely had more than one or two slaves. They used slaves for farming, but because the growing season was shorter and fewer crops could be raised, more slaves were used as house servants or to help in businesses. Slavery was expensive and not very profitable. Northern states began to outlaw it: first Vermont, in 1777, followed by Massachusetts and New Hampshire

Crispus Attucks

During the Boston Massacre on March 5, 1770, runaway slave Crispus Attucks led a small group in an attack on British soldiers. He was shot and killed, making him the first American to die in the fight for independence.

in 1783. Some states passed laws that freed slaves over time, or freed the children of slaves, such as Pennsylvania in 1780, Connecticut and Rhode Island in 1784, New York in 1799, and New Jersey in 1804. For some in northern states, however, their wait for freedom would not be over until federal abolition in 1865.

New England became a headquarters for abolitionists, such as Sojourner Truth's friend William Lloyd Garrison of Massachusetts. Garrison called the Constitution "a pact with hell" because slavery had been written into it. He founded the abolitionist newspaper *The Liberator* and helped establish the American Anti-Slavery Society in 1833. But writing and campaigning were not enough. Many abolitionists knew that politics would take too long to make real change for the millions of slaves that suffered in the South. They needed help *now*.

Presidential Slaves

George Washington kept a large plantation home, called Mount Vernon, in Virginia. He owned over 300 male slaves and untold numbers of women and children. His slave families lived together in crude huts, where husbands and wives slept on rough beds, their children on the dirt floor. He allowed his slaves to keep small personal gardens and to raise chickens that they could sell in town. Every week, each family received about 15 pounds of corn to eat, as well as 22 small fish each month.[1]

Washington kept slaves throughout his life, but after watching black soldiers fight bravely in the Revolutionary War, he changed his mind about slavery. In his will, he granted his 160 slaves their freedom upon his death. The rest of the Mount Vernon slaves belonged to his wife, Martha. Upon Martha's death, her slaves were split up among her grandchildren, which in some cases tore families apart.

Thomas Jefferson owned over 600 slaves over his lifetime.[2] He fell in love with one of them, Sarah "Sally" Hemings. They had several children together, all while Jefferson was married to his wife, Martha. Interestingly, Sally and Martha were half-sisters—Sally was the daughter of Betty Hemings, a slave girl, and Martha's father, John Wayles.

Jefferson believed strongly that white people were superior in all ways to blacks. In *Notes on the State of Virginia,* Jefferson wrote that blacks "are inferior to whites in the endowments of the body and mind." While whites, according to Jefferson, had "flowing hair," a "fine mixture of red and white" skin, and "a more elegant symmetry of form," blacks have "a very strong and disagreeable odor." He also believed that blacks were not as intelligent as whites, saying, "Never yet could I find that a black had uttered a thought above the level of plain narration; never see even an elementary trait, of painting or sculpture."[3]

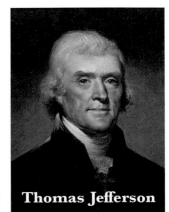

Thomas Jefferson

CHAPTER 4

SLAVERY IN THE SOUTH

Cotton grows well in the hot, sunny South. The bolls—balls of soft white fiber—stand out like snow in the summertime. But picking out the unwanted seeds hidden inside each tuft was slow work. Deseeding a pound of cotton took an entire day. A farmer could not make a profit using slaves that way, and in 1800, slavery was actually on the decline.

But around the same time, the price of raw cotton suddenly doubled. With Eli Whitney's invention of the cotton gin in 1793, one person could easily deseed ten pounds a day. U.S. cotton production skyrocketed, from 73,000 bales of cotton in 1800, or 9 percent of the world's supply, to 10 times that in 1820. By 1850, the United States was a global cotton leader, supplying 68 percent of the world's total.[1]

Southern plantation owners became rich and powerful thanks to cotton, the new "white gold." Cotton production was able to thrive because of the cheap labor of slaves. Slaves cut down the forests and drained the

Hand-powered engines, or gins, like this early roller gin, separated unwanted sticky green seeds from the soft cotton fibers.

Slaves plant sweet potatoes on James Hopkins's plantation in Edisto, South Carolina.

swamps of the frontier in the Deep South—Alabama, Mississippi, Louisiana—to lay claim to even more farmland. Where the land in backcountry South Carolina could yield 300 pounds of cotton in a single acre, in the rich soil of Alabama, farmers could grow 800 or even 1,000 pounds per acre.[2] Slavery grew to fill the new frontier: 1840—2.4 million slaves; 1850—3.2 million slaves; 1860—3.9 million slaves. Soon Natchez, Mississippi, boasted more millionaires than anywhere else on earth.[3] However, most Southerners were not well off. In fact, in 1860, less than 25 percent of Southerners owned even one slave.[4] Fewer than 3,000 owned one hundred or more. Those few who did had such a powerful influence over business and government that Southern society came to see having a slave as an important status symbol.

In the U.S. Congress, these wealthy Southern gentlemen proudly stood up for slavery. They argued viciously with Northern abolitionists. The new frontier states, as well as those to come, needed rules. Which states would allow slavery and

which would not? While slavery threatened to tear the country in two, millions of black slaves continued to suffer every day.

The overseer's horn sounded before sunrise even kissed the ground. Work time. The slaves shuffled quietly from their huts to the cotton field, wincing when they heard a scream. Someone who dared to sleep too late was getting whipped. There was just too much to do to rest, from the time the fields were first plowed in March or April until the harvest in August. The plantations are so large that by the time one round of hoeing was done, it was time to start all over again.[5]

Mothers and fathers parted ways from their youngest children. All day the grown folks plowed or hoed or weeded or picked. Sometimes the slave driver gave 10 or 15 minutes to eat a lunch, if the slaves were able to pack one—usually cold leftovers of bacon and corn pone. But then it was back to work, and every soul worked until the overseer blew the horn again at quitting time. Sometimes that was sunset; sometimes later. At harvest time, the slaves then brought their

The soft white bolls on this row of cotton plants stand ready for picking. Harvesting cotton by hand was a slow process, and often left the picker bloody and scratched by thorns and sharp twigs.

At the end of the day, slaves head out of the fields and toward the gin-house, hauling baskets piled high with freshly picked cotton.

cotton baskets to the gin-house for weighing. Every slave picked 200 pounds of cotton a day. Woe to the slave who picked more than that. Then the master would expect the same, or more, the next day.

Those who picked less were whipped—25 lashes, 50 lashes, or if they got caught sitting idle in the fields, 100 lashes.[6] Man or woman, off came their thin, ragged shirt. The overseer tied the slave belly-up against a tree, or with hands and feet bound to four posts on the ground. Out would come the angry whip. For a half second, all eyes watched it fly through the air before it landed, slicing open even the toughest back. How hard the people worked was no matter. The overseer often found a reason for screams to cut through the buzz of crickets.

Even after working the fields all day, slaves knew they could not rest yet. Ordinary chores waited. Men went to the stables to feed the mules and clean out the barn, or to the forest to chop wood for the Big House, where the master lived. In their own meager shacks on Slave Row, behind the plantation's Big House, women still had to cook dinner for their own families, sometimes the only meal all day. They made simple meals from the cornmeal, buttermilk, and bits of bacon or pickled fish the master handed out. At least then, families came together.

Mamas could hear about their young one's chores—picking apples in the orchard, washing dishes in the Big House, helping watch the master's new baby.

Then there were evening chores. Women made thread out of cotton, or yarn out of wool, or they sewed sack-cloth for her family's clothes or quilts out of rags for their bedding. It all had to be done before the morning.[7] When their hands could do no more, man, woman, and child sank into their small, hard beds, or even onto the dirt floor. Sleep was short and fitful. When they dreamed, they dreamed of how to survive tomorrow, how to avoid the whip.

Weekends could be special times. Saturday night, many plantation slaves got together to make music. They made quills, or tuned whistles, from short reeds cut and bundled together. They used metal buckets or wood planks as drums. They danced with their whole bodies, shaking the work out with the turkey trot, the buzzard lope, the Mary Jane. Children made marbles out of clay, dried them in the sun, and played. They might make stick horses, or they would build playhouses out of bark or reeds or just marked-off dirt.[8]

A slave family portrait, taken around 1862 on Smith's Plantation in Beaufort, South Carolina

Slave auctions were held in large towns where buyers could examine each slave up close. Slaves were chained to the auction block. They checked their teeth, muscles, and checked for any health problems. Traders used tricks on the buyers like dyeing black older slaves' gray hair. They applied grease to the slave's bodies to make them look healthier.

Sunday was a day to rest and go to church. Slaves who weren't too feeble had to walk miles to the nearest white church, watching their masters roll down the lane in carriages. White and black folks went to the same church, but sat far apart, sometimes with slaves outside in the heat listening to the preaching until the afternoon. Afterward, the black folks stayed and had a picnic on the church lawn. Sometimes stories of the Bible, shared with friends, seemed like their only escape. Spiritual songs, low and slow, could soothe a troubled soul.

Often, slaves tried to hold their own prayer meetings, after dark, in the woods. In these secret times, they sang, prayed, and plotted. They taught each other how to read; they dared to plan escapes. These meetings were against the law. To even leave the plantation required a written pass from the master. Savage punishments awaited those who tried to escape—branding with a hot iron, cutting off their ears, or slashing their Achilles tendon so that they could not run. Still, hope remained—some did escape to a life of freedom in the North.

Auction Day

Many slaves could expect to be sold at least once in their lifetime, if not several times. They could be sold if their master ran out of money. Some were sold because they were disobedient. Some plantation owners were slave breeders. They bought healthy female slaves and sold their babies, taking them as soon as they were old enough to stand.[9] Sometimes neighboring farmers sold to one another, but more often slave traders controlled sales. Confederate General Nathan Bedford Forrest, one of the most successful slave traders, made $96,000 in profit in a single year in the 1850s from his Memphis, Tennessee—based business.[10]

Slaves with different qualities brought different prices. Guy and Andrew were sold at the largest auction in U.S. history in 1859. Both were rated as A1–Prime Hand—the best field hands. Guy was bought for $1,240, while Andrew, who had lost his right eye, was bought for $200 less.[11] Today, these prices would be equivalent to $33,000 to $40,000.

Young and pretty women, who would make good house slaves, also fetched a high price. So did strong women who could work in the field, or those who had already had healthy babies that their owners could sell. Values decreased from a ¾ hand to a ¼ hand, to zero for elderly slaves or slaves with physical or mental illnesses. Mothers and children were often sold separately, with no guarantee they would ever see each other again.

Slaves wait to be sold at an auction in 1853 in Virginia.

CHAPTER 5

WHICH PATH LEADS TO FREEDOM?

With the odds stacked against them, how could slaves become free? In the early days of slavery, some bought their own freedom from their owners. As the 1800s marched on, however, and the value of slaves skyrocketed, it became difficult for a slave to scrape together enough money to afford himself.

A slave could try to find his freedom on foot—by running away. Few attempted the dangerous journey and lived. There was no single known path to freedom, no well-known signals or signs to follow. Slaves most often ran alone, at night, through unfamiliar forests and swamps, where they risked getting injured or lost. Some runaways got scared and returned to their masters, even though they knew they could face any number of brutal punishments. If a slave could escape to a free state, he or she *could* become free for life. But there were no guarantees. Because of the Fugitive Slave Act of 1850, even slaves who had successfully escaped to the North could be dragged back into chains if their masters found them.

A runaway slave faced a dangerous and often lonely journey, with few places to hide or rest.

Levi Coffin

Some whites and free blacks broke the law and secretly aided runaways. John Fairfield, the son of a Virginia slaveowner, disguised himself as a slave trader when in fact he was taking "his" slaves to freedom.[1] Levi Coffin hid runaway slaves in his businesses and houses in Indiana and Ohio. But most often, if runaways got help, it was from other runaways. Harriet Tubman was born in 1820, a slave on a Maryland cotton plantation. When she ran away to freedom in Pennsylvania in 1849, she had to run alone. Heartbroken, Tubman worried about her still-enslaved family. She worked as a maid to save money to help them run away, too. But Tubman didn't stop after freeing her family. She risked her life again and again to return at least 19 times to lead as many as 300 slaves to safety in the North.[2]

Tubman, Fairfield, Coffin, and others were "conductors" on the Underground Railroad. Each one risked his or her freedom to help tens or even hundreds of slaves find theirs. In total, as many as 100,000 slaves escaped the South.[3] They were the lucky ones, making up a very small percentage of the millions of blacks who would never know freedom.

Another successful runaway was Frederick Douglass. Douglass's education made him rare among blacks and helped him blend in as he made his journey to

Harriet Tubman

freedom. As a free man, he traveled all over the country to tell others the truth about slavery. Douglass wrote a best-selling autobiography and published an abolitionist newspaper, *The North Star*. White abolitionists had been around for a while, but their support was small. With Douglass speaking about his actual experience, the abolition movement gained steam.

By the time Abraham Lincoln ran for president in 1860, Douglass had helped make the abolition of slavery into a national discussion. He even debated with Lincoln at the White House.

Frederick Douglass

Dred Scott

Other slaves, like Dred Scott, hoped that the law would be on their side. Scott grew up a slave, serving Peter Blow and his family in Virginia. When Blow died after moving to Missouri, Scott faced the auction block in a slave market in St. Louis. He was bought by a surgeon with the U.S. Army, Dr. John Emerson. A busy man, Emerson needed Scott to be a butler—someone to mend his clothes, make his bed, prepare meals, split wood. It was a gentler life than that of a field hand in Virginia.

Dr. Emerson's work in the Army kept him busy and traveling, and Scott went with him. They moved from fort to fort

Dred and Harriet Scott made their home in this room at Fort Snelling, near St. Paul, Minnesota.

around the northern Mississippi River, from St. Louis, Missouri, to Fort Armstrong in Illinois, and finally to Fort Snelling in the Wisconsin Territory, where they remained until 1840. They eventually returned to St. Louis, but Dr. Emerson died soon after. Scott offered Mrs. Emerson $300 to buy freedom for himself and his wife. Mrs. Emerson refused.

Missouri was a slave state, but Scott knew the law. Because he had been a resident of Illinois and the Wisconsin Territory, both free lands, he was entitled to his freedom. Scott sued Mrs. Emerson for his freedom and won. Then, unexpectedly, the Missouri Supreme Court reversed this decision and gave the Scotts back to Mrs. Emerson.

The Scotts refused to give up. Ten years after the original lawsuit was filed, Dred Scott's case was heard before the U.S. Supreme Court. Five of the nine Supreme Court justices were slaveholders; the Chief Justice, Roger Taney, was a fierce supporter of slavery. On March 6, 1857, the Court decided, 7-2, that because Dred and Harriet Scott were black, they were not citizens at all, of any state. The decision thrilled slaveholders throughout the South, but angered many in the North. The Dred Scott Decision would set back the efforts of abolitionists and antislavery activists. Dred Scott had tried to follow the law, but the law seemed to twist away from the problems of black slaves. Some came to believe in a simpler solution—violence.

Nat Turner was a trusted slave in the house of Joseph Travis of Southampton County, Virginia. At an early age, his mistress used the Bible to teach him how to read, and from it, he found his calling. He met with nearby slaves in secret, preaching that God had chosen him to avenge the sins of slavery. Other slaves joined his cause. Together they plotted a rebellion for August 21, 1831.

Early in the morning of August 21, Turner unlatched the door to his master's house. Six slaves wielding axes killed Joseph Travis, his wife, Sally, their son, their baby, and a twelve-year-old apprentice as they slept. The rebels moved quickly from home to home, slaughtering every white person they encountered. Other slaves joined in bloody parade, and within two days, 57 whites—including 46 women and children—were dead.[4]

The slave rebellion gathered steam as Turner's band headed for Jerusalem, Virginia. Panicked whites hid or ran for their lives. It took one week, 2,000 local militiamen, and 800 U.S. Army troops to bring order and capture more than 50 rebels. Nat Turner was a fugitive for nearly two months until a farmer discovered him in a barn on October 31. He was hanged for his crimes on November 11.

Nat Turner schemes with supporters.

John Brown believed that only a rebellion could stop slavery. He was willing to kill and to die for the cause.

Slaveholders had seen slaves kill before. Gabriel Prosser was hanged in 1800 alongside his two brothers and 23 other slaves for plotting a revolt near Richmond, Virginia. Denmark Vesey, a free black and former slave, was hanged with five other slaves in 1822 for plotting to kill slaveholders in Charleston, South Carolina.

Some white abolitionists also took up their cause. Both George Boxley in 1815 and John Brown in 1859 said they heard orders from heaven to free the slaves. They tried to lead slaves in rebellion, but both times, their plots failed.

Again and again, slaveholders stamped out these rebellions, with the local and the national government on their side. Still, every slave dreamed of a day when they would all be free. How could they make that dream come true?

As part of a slave revolt? That brought only death. Whites took revenge after each rebellion, killing blacks in retaliation.

In a court of law? The law rarely favored the slaves. When it did, lawsuits only worked for the few slaves who could read and write, or who had the support of powerful white friends.

Buying freedom? With what money, when the master let them have and earn so little?

Until that day when all people would be free, one last, risky option gave a slave hope.

Run.

The Colonization Plan

Chief Justice Roger Taney decreed in *Dred Scott v. Sanford:* "The black race for more than a century has been regarded as beings of an inferior order, and they have no rights which the white man is bound to respect." Few could guess that Justice Taney himself had freed his own slaves.[5] Not that he believed his slaves should be free in the United States—Taney had other plans. He and many other whites, including Thomas Jefferson and politician Henry Clay, felt that the white race and the black race could never live together peacefully. They believed that blacks would never have the same advantages in society or politics as whites.

These men were a different kind of abolitionist, the kind that formed the American Colonization Society in 1817.[6] They supported the controversial idea that freed black slaves should be shipped back to Africa. In 1822, the Society established a colony on Africa's west coast, a place where former slaves could establish a government of their own. The Society sent a new group of black immigrants each year. They also sent white missionaries to help "civilize" the native Africans and convert them to Christianity. By 1858, the colony had swelled to a population of 11,172, two-thirds of which were former slaves.

In 1847, the Society renamed the colony the Republic of Liberia. They helped set up an American-style government, naming its capital city Monrovia, after former U.S. president James Monroe, also a colonization supporter. The colony survived to become the modern-day country of Liberia.

Chief Justice Roger Taney

1619   The first slaves arrive in the British colony of Virginia, brought by a Dutch ship.

1770   Crispus Attucks, a runaway slave, becomes the first American to die in the Revolutionary War.

1773   Phillis Wheatley's collection of poems is published in London.

1787   The U.S. Constitution is ratified with special protections for slavery. Its signers agree that each slave counts only as 3/5ths of a person.

1793   Eli Whitney invents the cotton gin, making it easier and faster to remove seeds from harvested cotton.

1797   Isabella Baumfree (later known as Sojourner Truth) is born to slave parents in rural New York.

1817   The American Colonization Society is formed.

1831   Nat Turner leads a bloody slave rebellion in Virginia in August. William Lloyd Garrison publishes the first issue of the abolitionist newspaper *The Liberator.*

1839   Joseph Cinqué leads 52 Africans to take control of the slave ship *Lá Amistad.*

1841   Solomon Northrup, a free black from New York, is sold into slavery in Louisiana.

1847   The African colony for former slaves is named the Republic of Liberia.

1849   Harriet Tubman escapes to freedom the first time.

1850   The United States supplies nearly 70% of the world's cotton. The Fugitive Slave Act is passed.

1852   Harriet Beecher Stowe publishes *Uncle Tom's Cabin.*

1857   The U.S. Supreme Court rules that blacks cannot be citizens of the United States in *Dred Scott vs. Sanford.*

1859   John Brown and his sons try and fail to lead a slave rebellion in Harper's Ferry, Virginia.

1860   Abraham Lincoln is elected president. South Carolina secedes from the Union.

1861   The first shots of the Civil War are fired.

1863   Abraham Lincoln signs the Emancipation Proclamation. The presidential decree frees slaves in Confederate states.

1865   The Confederacy surrenders, ending the Civil War. President Lincoln is shot and killed by John Wilkes Booth. States ratify the 13th Amendment, banning slavery in the United States.

1868   States ratify the 14th Amendment, granting full citizenship to blacks.

Chapter 1. Bought and Sold

1. "The Kidnapping Case: Narrative of the Seizure and Recovery of Solomon Northup," *The New York Times,* January 20, 1853.

Chapter 2. Slavery Comes to America

1. Julius Lester, *To Be a Slave* (New York: Dial Press, 1968), pp. 18–19.

2. Ibid., p. 21.

3. Ibid., p. 22.

4. Henry Louis Gates, Jr., "How Many Slaves Landed in the U.S.?" *Americans: Many Rivers to Cross,* PBS. http://www.pbs.org/wnet/african-americans-many-rivers-to-cross/history/how-many-slaves-landed-in-the-us/

5. John Hope Franklin and Alfred Moss, Jr., *From Slavery to Freedom: A History of Negro Americans,* 6th Ed. (New York: McGraw-Hill, 1988), pp. 25–26.

6. Gates.

7. Franklin and Moss, p. 52.

Chapter 3. Slavery in the North

1. Julius Lester, *To Be a Slave* (New York: Dial Press, 1968), p. 63.

2. Henry Wiencek, "The Dark Side of Thomas Jefferson," *Smithsonian Magazine,* October 2012, http://www.smithsonianmag.com/history/the-dark-side-of-thomas-jefferson-35976004/?no-ist=&page=3

3. Thomas Jefferson, "Notes on the State of Virginia," *Africans in America,* PBS, http://www.pbs.org/wgbh/aia/part3/3h490t.html

Chapter 4. Slavery in the South

1. Daniel Walker Howe, *What Hath God Wrought: The Transformation of America, 1815–1848* (Oxford, UK: Oxford University Press, 2007), p. 128.

2. Ibid.

3. "Division," *America: The History of Us,* The History Channel, May 2, 2010.

4. Julius Lester, *To Be a Slave* (New York: Dial Press, 1968), p. 60.

5. Ibid., p. 66.

6. Ibid., p. 72.

7. Belinda Hurmence, *Slavery Time When I Was Chillun* (New York: G. P. Putnam's Sons, 1997), p. 11.

8. Ibid., p. 5.

9. Lester, p. 39.

10. Ibid., p. 43.

11. Daina Ramey Berry, "Four Myths About Slavery in the U.S.," *RawStory,* October 21, 2014, http://www.rawstory.com/rs/2014/10/four-myths-about-slavery-in-the-us/

Chapter 5. Which Path Leads to Freedom?

1. John Hope Franklin and Alfred Moss, Jr., *From Slavery to Freedom: A History of Negro Americans,* 6th Ed. (New York: McGraw-Hill, 1988), p. 171.

2. Ibid., pp. 171–172.

3. Ibid., 172.

4. Daniel Walker Howe, *What Hath God Wrought: The Transformation of America, 1815–1848* (Oxford, UK: Oxford University Press, 2007), p. 324.

5. Ibid., p. 442.

6. Vermont Historical Society, "Underground Railroad Project: Colonization Movement," http://vermonthistory.org/educate/online-resources/underground-railroad-project/colonization-movement

Books

Anderson, Laurie Halse. *Chains*. New York: Atheneum Books for Young Readers, 2010.

Fradin, Judith Bloom, and Dennis Brindell Fradin. *Stolen into Slavery: The True Story of Solomon Northup, Free Black Man*. Washington, DC: National Geographic, 2014.

Grady, Cynthia. *I Lay My Stitches Down: Poems of American Slavery*. Grand Rapids, Michigan: Eerdmans Books for Young Readers, 2011.

Kamma, Anne. *If You Lived When There Was Slavery in America*. New York: Scholastic Press, 2004.

McKissack, Patricia C. *A Picture of Freedom: The Diary of Clotee, a Slave Girl, Belmont Plantation, Virginia 1859*. New York: Scholastic Press, 2011.

Slavery: Real People and Their Stories of Enslavement. Edited by Jo Bourne. London: DK Books, 2009.

On the Internet

Frederick Douglass National Historical Site
    http://www.nps.gov/frdo/learn/historyculture/people.htm

Remembering Slavery: Those Who Survived Tell Their Stories. Ed. Jeutonne Brewer, University of North Carolina–Greensboro
    http://www.uncg.edu/~jpbrewer/remember/

Slave Memories. "Slavery and the Making of America." PBS
    http://www.pbs.org/wnet/slavery/memories/index_flash.html

Slavery in America. National Museum of American History, Smithsonian Institution
    http://americanhistory.si.edu/changing-america-emancipation-proclamation-1863-and-march-washington-1963/1863/slavery-america

Cotton fields

FIND OUT MORE

Works Consulted

Berry, Daina Ramey. "Four Myths About Slavery in the U.S." *RawStory,* October 21, 2014. http://www.rawstory.com/rs/2014/10/four-myths-about-slavery-in-the-us/

"Division." *America: The History of Us.* The History Channel, May 2, 2010.

Franklin, John Hope, and Alfred A. Moss, Jr. *From Slavery to Freedom: A History of Negro Americans. 6th Ed.* New York: McGraw-Hill, 1988.

Gates, Henry Louis, Jr. "How Many Slaves Landed in the U.S.?" *Americans: Many Rivers to Cross.* PBS. http://www.pbs.org/wnet/african-americans-many-rivers-to-cross/history/how-many-slaves-landed-in-the-us/

Howe, Daniel Walker. *What Hath God Wrought: The Transformation of America, 1815–1848.* Oxford, UK: Oxford University Press, 2007.

Hurmence, Belinda. *Slavery Time When I Was Chillun.* New York: G. P. Putnam's Sons, 1997.

Jefferson, Thomas. "Notes on the State of Virginia." *Africans in America.* PBS, http://www.pbs.org/wgbh/aia/part3/3h490t.html.

"The Kidnapping Case: Narrative of the Seizure and Recovery of Solomon Northup." *The New York Times,* January 20, 1853. http://query.nytimes.com/mem/archive-free/pdf?res=9E03EEDC1438E334BC4851DFB7668388649FDE&smid=nytimesarts

Lester, Julius. *To Be a Slave.* New York: Dial Press, 1968.

Vermont Historical Society. "Colonization Movement." http://vermonthistory.org/educate/online-resources/underground-railroad-project/colonization-movement

Wiencek, Henry. "The Dark Side of Thomas Jefferson." *Smithsonian Magazine,* October 2012. http://www.smithsonianmag.com/history/the-dark-side-of-thomas-jefferson-35976004/?no-ist=&page=3

abolitionist (ah-boh-LIH-shuh-nist)—A person who wanted slavery to be outlawed.

auction (AWK-shun)—A public sale where each item is sold to the person who offers the most money.

branding—Burning with a hot iron to make a permanent mark.

caboceer (kah-buh-SEE-er)—An African who worked with his chief to sell free Africans to European slave traders.

cash crop—A plant grown for the purpose of selling, usually in large quantities.

cat-o'-nine-tails (kat-oh-NYN-taylz)—A whip made from nine knotted cords joined at a single handle.

colonization (kah-luh-nih-ZAY-shun)—The settling of a new territory.

compromise (KAHM-proh-myz)—An agreement between two arguing sides, where each gets part of what they want.

dialect (DY-uh-lekt)—A manner of speaking a language that is specific to a certain region.

Middle Passage—The journey across the Atlantic Ocean, from the west coast of Africa to America, to deliver human cargo into slavery.

overseer (OH-ver-see-er)—A man put in charge of laboring slaves.

plantation (plan-TAY-shun)—A large farm.

rebellion (ree-BEL-yun)—Resistance to the government or to people in charge.

revolt (ree-VOLT)—To break away from or rise up against people in charge.